USBORNE COMPUTER GUIDES

COMPUTERS
FOR BEGINNERS

Margaret Stephens & Rebecca Treays

Edited by
Philippa Wingate & Jane Chisholm

Designed by Russell Punter

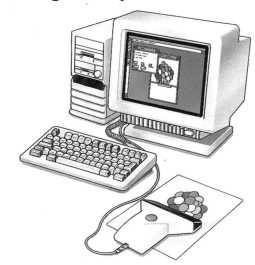

Additional designs by Robert Walster

Illustrated by Colin Mier & Sean Wilkinson
Additional illustrations by Kuo Kang Chen & Peter Dennis

Technical consultant: Dr. Ian Brown

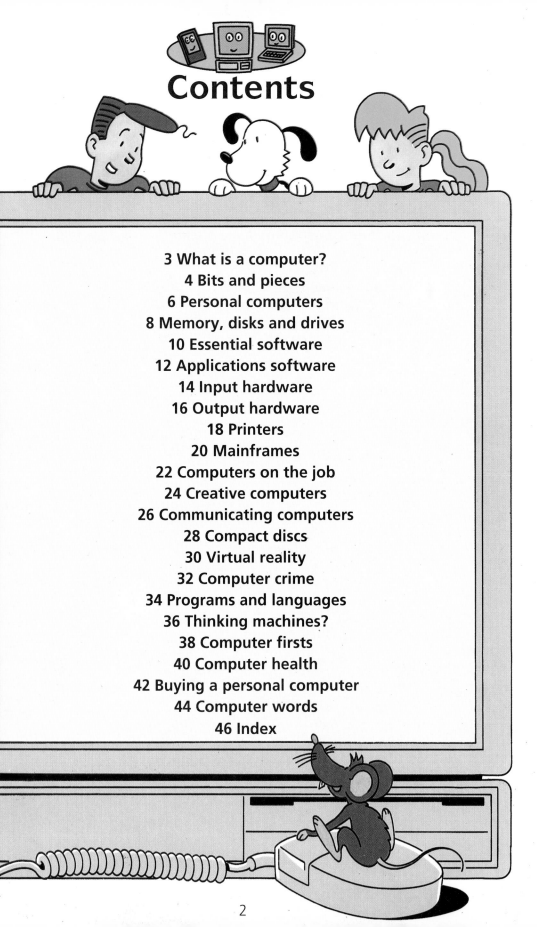

Contents

3 What is a computer?
4 Bits and pieces
6 Personal computers
8 Memory, disks and drives
10 Essential software
12 Applications software
14 Input hardware
16 Output hardware
18 Printers
20 Mainframes
22 Computers on the job
24 Creative computers
26 Communicating computers
28 Compact discs
30 Virtual reality
32 Computer crime
34 Programs and languages
36 Thinking machines?
38 Computer firsts
40 Computer health
42 Buying a personal computer
44 Computer words
46 Index

What is a computer?

A computer takes in facts, known as **data** and, following instructions, it processes these facts to produce information. Computers can process vast amounts of data in a very short time. Your brain can do this too.

A computer cannot think for itself. It will do exactly as it is told - no more and no less. People often talk about "computer error", but usually this means human error. If you're sent a computerized electricity bill for millions of dollars when you only use one light bulb, it means that the computer has been given the wrong instructions.

In order to process data, computers need two things - hardware and software. **Hardware** is the computer's machinery - the parts you can see and touch, like the monitor and all the electronic devices and circuits inside it. **Software** is all the facts and the lists of instructions that a computer receives in order to carry out its tasks. All the different lists of instructions are called **programs**.

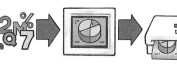

Data   Computer   Information

Data and information can be numbers, letters, sounds, pictures or symbols. Pictures and symbols which a computer produces are called **graphics**.

What happens inside

This picture shows what goes on inside the brain of your computer - its processing unit .

Input (data and instructions) is fed into the computer.

The *control unit*. Input comes here first and is sent to the correct part of the computer to be processed. When work is completed, the control unit collects the information.

The *arithmetic unit*. The computer carries out all its work here. The control unit and the arithmetic unit are together called the *Central Processing Unit* (CPU).

Memory. Data and instructions are stored here.

Output, the processed data, is delivered to the user.

Bits and pieces

All the data and instructions inside a computer are stored and processed as numbers. Most computers use only two digits: 0 and 1. This is called **binary code**. 0 and 1 are called **binary digits**, or **bits** for short.

Although it is hard to believe, all sorts of information, from pictures and photographs to words and music, can be stored as patterns of just these two numbers.

Inside the computer, the digits 0 and 1 are recorded as pulses of electricity on tiny electronic circuits. If a circuit is carrying an electrical pulse, it is a 1, if not, it is a 0. All the input fed into a computer has to be coded as a different combination of pulses and non-pulses.

Morse is another kind of binary code. Letters and numbers become a series of long or short sounds, known as dots and dashes.

Bits and bytes

Pieces of computer data are stored in series of eight bits called **bytes.**

The letter B is converted to the byte 01000010.

Letter B

Bit

Byte

Computer logic

To process data, a computer sends electrical pulses through electronic circuits. A circuit is made up of a system of electronic pathways and electronic devices called **logic gates**. As each pulse passes through a gate, it may be changed to a non-pulse. This is the way data is processed. Gates are arranged in thousands of different patterns which can add, subtract, compare, memorize and do all the other work inside a computer.

Silicon chips

Electronic circuits are stored on chips. **Chips** are tiny slices of a substance called silicon. Each chip is covered with millions of circuits. The way circuits are arranged decides what jobs each chip can do. So, for example, there are special chips for the memory of a computer and one for its CPU. All the chips in a computer are mounted on boards called **printed circuit boards (PCBs).**

A printed circuit board from a personal computer

Narrow bands of metal printed on the board carry electricity to the chips.

CPU chip

Some chips are so small they can pass through the eye of a needle.

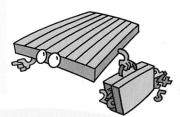

Chips with everything

Many modern machines contain chips. Here are some examples.

Washing machine

Battleships game

Industrial robot

Electronic keyboard

Smaller PCBs, called *daughterboards,* can be attached to the motherboard.

Memory chips

The main PCB inside a PC is called the *motherboard.*

Buses

Information flows around the computer in bytes. Bytes are carried along metal paths called **buses**. Every bus consists of several tracks, and each track carries one bit. There are three types of bus: the data bus, the control bus and the address bus.

Data buses

A **data bus** carries data between the CPU and the memory, or between the CPU and an input or output device (see pages 14-19).

Control buses

A **control bus** carries instructions from the CPU to other parts of the computer. For example, a signal can be sent from the CPU telling the memory whether a piece of data is to be stored there or taken out.

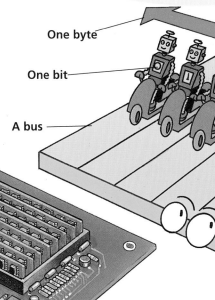

One byte

One bit

A bus

Address buses

An **address bus** carries the numbers (addresses) which identify each place in the computer's memory.

Personal computers

A **personal computer** (often called a **PC**) is a small machine that fits onto a desk and can be used by one person. Today, personal computers are almost as familiar as televisions and ballpoint pens. There are many millions of them in use throughout the world. This is amazing when you think that the first personal computer wasn't available until 1971.

Before personal computers were developed, all computers were mainframes (see page 20). Mainframes are large and expensive and were only used by big organizations. Personal computers became popular because they were small and cost less than one percent of the price of a mainframe.

Since the mid 1980s, personal computers have become even smaller and even cheaper, as well as much more powerful.

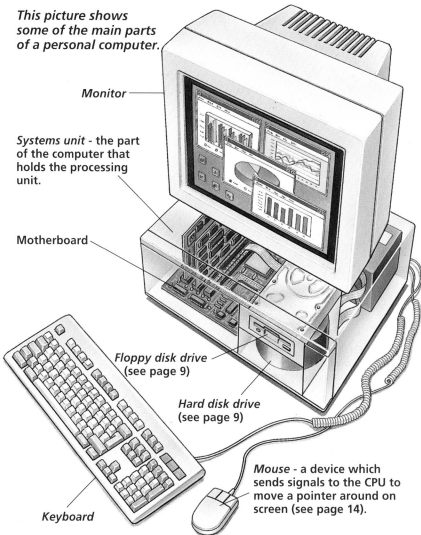

This picture shows some of the main parts of a personal computer.

Monitor

Systems unit - the part of the computer that holds the processing unit.

Motherboard

Floppy disk drive (see page 9)

Hard disk drive (see page 9)

Mouse - a device which sends signals to the CPU to move a pointer around on screen (see page 14).

Keyboard

Key dates in the history of personal computers

1950-70 Mainframe computers are used in large organizations.

1971 With the development of the chip, computers become much smaller.

The first PC is sold for individual use. It didn't have its own monitor, but used a television screen.

1975 The first PC with a screen and keyboard

is sold in kit form. It is named the *Altair*, after a planet in the TV series *Star Trek*.

1977 The first ready-made PCs with screens and keyboards are produced.

1979 First software program for PC users is designed. This enabled everyone to work with personal computers, not only experts who could write their own programs.

Portables

During the 1980s, personal computers were developed that were small enough to be picked up. These are called **portables**.

The biggest portables weigh about 7kg (15lb). That's about the weight of a young baby, so they are not that easy to carry. Older models needed electricity, so they could be used only where there was an electrical socket.

A notebook computer

Notebook computers often weigh less than 3kg (6lb) and are useful for people who need to write letters, take notes, or make calculations on the move. But their keyboards and monitors are very small and can be awkward to use. Notebooks have rechargeable batteries which last about three hours.

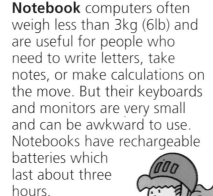

A **PDA (Personal Digital Assistant)** is so tiny it can fit into the palm of your hand. The most up-to-date PDAs can run spreadsheet, database and word processing software (see pages 12-13).

The Newton, made by Apple

One of the smallest PDAs is a notepad. It is like a computerized note pad. Notes and sketches drawn on the screen with a special pen are converted into text and diagrams.

1981 IBM, a US company, brings out its first PC. Soon many other companies design personal computers based on the IBM PC. The similarity between these machines means that different brands of PCs can communicate with each other (see page 26).

1983 Apple produces the *Macintosh,* a PC with a mouse. It introduces the use of graphics.

1997 Many million of PCs are in use throughout the world. Many people are buying them for their homes. As technology develops, models become smaller and smaller.

A PDA computer

Memory, disks and drives

Memory is the place in a computer where information can be stored. Memory is made up of chips. Every computer has two kinds of memory: Read-Only Memory (ROM) and Random-Access Memory (RAM).

RAM

Random-Access Memory stores data and instructions while the computer is turned on. It is called Random-Access Memory because the computer can pick out, or access, any piece of data from any point.

RAM is only a temporary memory. When the computer is switched off all the data stored in it is lost.

ROM

Read-Only Memory holds a store of programs which tell the computer how to work. When the computer is first turned on and it is starting up (or **"booting up"**, as it is called in computer jargon), instructions from ROM tell the CPU how to get going.

As the name suggests, programs in ROM can only be read. The instructions cannot be changed, and they won't be wiped out when the computer is turned off.

Memory cells

Memory is divided into units called **cells** which can hold one byte of data. Each cell has an **address** so the CPU knows where a piece of data is stored.

It helps to think of memory as a series of pigeonholes. Each pigeonhole is a cell and each label is its address.

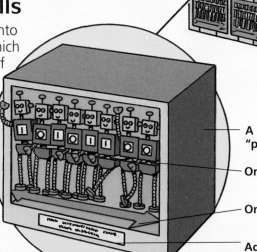

A group of cells

A single cell or "pigeonhole"

One bit

One byte

Address or "label"

Disks

To keep the information in RAM when your computer is turned off, you need to save it on a disk. **Optical discs** are the newest kind (see page 28), but most people use magnetic disks.

Magnetic disks are round pieces of plastic or metal, coated with a magnetic substance. Data, which is stored in RAM as pulses and non-pulses, is stored on these disks as magnetic or non-magnetic areas.

A device called a **disk drive** spins the disk, while **read/write heads** read or write data onto it. There are two types of magnetic disks: floppy and hard.

Floppy disks

Floppy disks are made of flexible plastic. They are usually covered with a hard plastic jacket, so they don't look floppy at all. You put them into and take them out of the disk drive yourself. Most floppy disks are 3.5 inches in size.

3.5 inch floppy disk

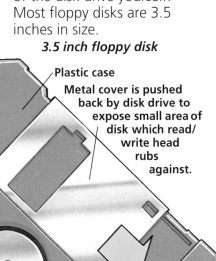

Plastic case

Metal cover is pushed back by disk drive to expose small area of disk which read/ write head rubs against.

Disk hub

Disk drive attaches itself to a hole in disk hub and spins disk.

Write-protect tab - when uncovered, no new data can be written onto disk.

Hard disks

Hard disks are made of glass or metal and live permanently inside the computer. They do exactly the same as floppy disks, except that they store more data and spin more quickly and, unlike floppies, you can't lose your hard disks.

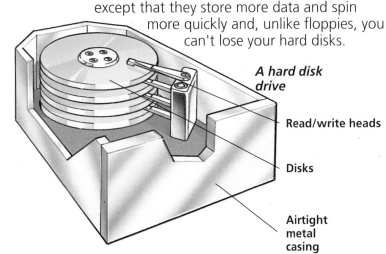

A hard disk drive

Read/write heads

Disks

Airtight metal casing

Magnetic tape

Data can also be stored on tape, similar to that used in cassettes for music. Like disks, tape is coated with magnetic iron oxide.

Tape cassettes are useful for storing lots of information, but they are not so good for everyday use. You have to wind all the way through them to find the data you need.

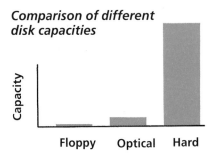

Capacity

The amount of data that can be stored in memory or on a disk is called its **capacity**. It is measured in megabytes (MB) (1,048,576 bytes) or gigabytes (GB) (1024 MB). Higher capacity disks are becoming more common.

Comparison of different disk capacities

Capacity

Floppy   Optical   Hard

Essential software

Software isn't soft. In fact, it cannot be touched or felt at all. All the information and instructions that make up software are rather like all the thoughts and ideas in your head. You can touch your head, but you cannot touch your thoughts.

Some instructions are built into the computer when it is manufactured and are permanently stored in ROM. This software "boots up" the computer when it is first turned on. The last part of the booting up process is to search the hard disk (or floppy disk, if there is no hard disk) for some vital software

called the **operating system**. The operating system allows the computer to do all the other jobs you want it to. Without it, your computer wouldn't be able to follow programs, called **applications software**, which are written for specific tasks.

Operating system

An **operating system** is a series of programs which organizes and controls a computer. Here are some of the things it does.

Controls the operation of applications software.

Organizes the hard and floppy disks, so they can store data.

Controls the hardware, such as the keyboard, the printer and the screen.

Controls the processes that store data on disks and take data from disks.

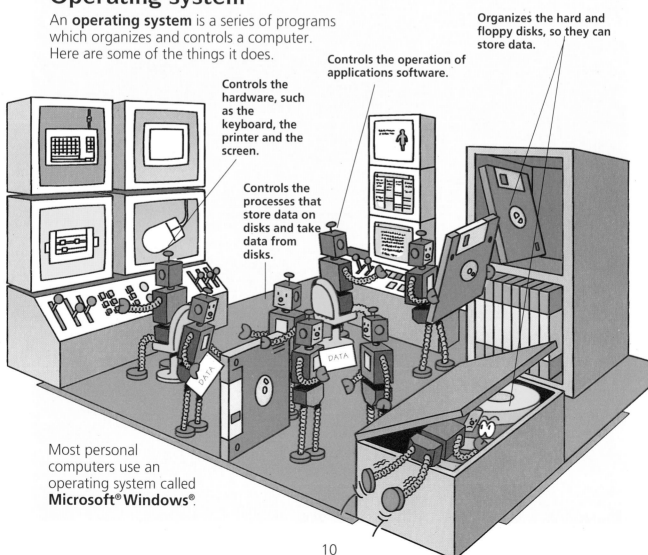

Most personal computers use an operating system called **Microsoft® Windows®**.

An operating system at work

This shows what happens inside your computer when you want to check a document for spelling mistakes:

1. The spellcheck command is selected with the keyboard or the mouse.

2. The CPU runs the operating system, which interprets the command.

3. The operating system finds the spellcheck software on the hard disk and loads it into RAM.

4. If there is no space in RAM, the operating system removes some data from RAM and places it temporarily on the hard disk. This process is called *swapping*.

5. Once in RAM, the CPU can follow the spellcheck instructions and correct your document.

Utility programs

On personal computers all information is organized into **files** (sometimes called **documents**). These files are themselves organized into groups called **folders** or **directories**. The operating system has special programs called **utilities** for keeping collections of files and folders tidy. Utilities allow you to name and rename files; you can also copy, delete, and regroup files.

Chips again

The software in ROM that boots up your computer when it is turned on is actually built into the ROM chips. The tiny circuits on each chip are specially designed so they represent binary code and are themselves sets of instructions. This means the software is also hardware, because the circuits are physical things you can see and touch. These ROM chips are called **firmware**.

Applications software

There are thousands and thousands of different types of applications software, covering almost every activity imaginable. There are programs for farmers, programs for gamblers, programs for games and programs for figuring out scientific formulas. New programs are being developed all the time. Some of the most used applications are described here.

Applications software packages usually contain a CD or a number of floppy disks and an instruction manual.

Word processing software

Word processing software allows you to type documents, such as letters or essays, onto the computer's screen. It includes many useful functions that make this easier. When a document is finished, you can store it on the computer's hard disk, or on a floppy disk.

These are some of the things a word processing program can do.

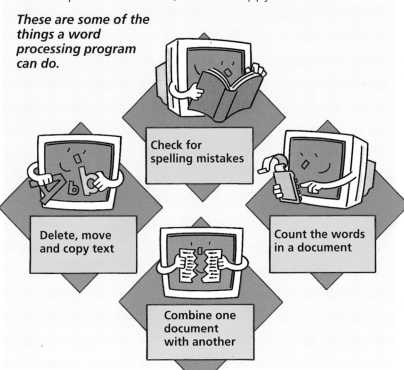

Check for spelling mistakes

Delete, move and copy text

Count the words in a document

Combine one document with another

Database software

A **database** is an electronic way of storing information. People have always tried to store information in a way that makes it easy to find what they want. For example, a restaurant guide is arranged according to the sort of food served. So, if you felt like eating Peking duck, you would flick through the "Chinese" pages.

But there may be other things you want to take into account, such as where the restaurant is and how much it charges. It could take quite a long time until you found one in the right place and at the right price. Using a database, you can type in all your requirements, and a list of the restaurants that suit you will appear on the screen.

Many companies keep information about their customers on a database.

Name: Anna Log

Each fact stored in a database has a label or *field*. The field for "Anna Log" is "Name".

Spreadsheet software

Spreadsheet software is used for figuring out money matters. It organizes figures into rows and columns, so they are clearly set out and easy to read, and it can add and subtract at high speed.

Spreadsheets are useful for predicting how much a business will make (its income), and what it will spend, in a year. This is called **forecasting**.

An example of how spreadsheets can be used is shown below.

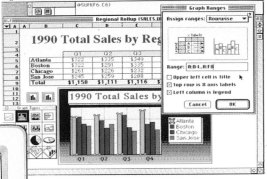

The picture above shows a spreadsheet displayed on a monitor.

Cost of item	25.00	Cost of item	30.00
Items sold	630	Items sold	567
Income	15,750.00	Income	17,010.00
Production	2,102.67	Production	2,102.67
Advertising	1,050.00	Advertising	1,050.00
Wages	3,450.00	Wages	3,450.00
Total costs	6,602.67	Total costs	6,602.67
Income	15,750.00	Income	17,010.00
- Costs	6,602.67	- Costs	6,602.67
= Profit	**9,147.33**	**= Profit**	**10,407.33**

The owner of a clothing business wants to sell jeans more cheaply than her rivals. But she still wants to make a profit of over $10,000. By entering details of different prices, how many she expects to sell at those prices and all the expenses involved in making them, she can figure out the cheapest price.

Fields about the same subject together make up a *record*.

A collection of records with the same fields makes up a *file*. A group of files makes up a database.

Integrated software

Integrated software combines a number of applications in one package. The most common type for a personal computer would be a combination of word processing, a database and a spreadsheet.

It is often cheaper to buy an integrated software package than to buy all the individual applications separately.

Input hardware

The data and instructions that a computer receives are called **input.** The hardware that receives them is called **input hardware**. Input hardware is like your sense organs (ears, eyes, nose etc) which take in information and send it to your brain.

Keyboards

The most common way to enter data into a computer is by **keyboard**. With word processing software, keyboards can be used to type documents and to send instructions to the CPU. But unless you are a very quick typist, keyboards are quite a slow way of sending commands. If you work too long at a keyboard (or a mouse) you can strain your wrists and other joints (see page 40).

A keyboard

Function keys can be programmed to send specific commands to the CPU.

A mouse

A **mouse** is a hand-operated input device. If you use your imagination, it does actually look like a real mouse. A mouse can be used to move a cursor (a pointer) around the screen, to draw shapes or to make a choice from a **menu**. (A menu is a list of different options.)

A mouse is usually made of plastic, and is often connected to the computer by a cable (its tail). On its underside is a metal or rubber ball, which moves as the mouse is dragged over a surface. The movement of the ball is converted into data, which is sent to the CPU.

The CPU uses this data to plot the direction of the mouse's movement. It sends signals to the pointer on the monitor screen, which follows the movement of the mouse exactly.

How a mouse works

1. As the ball rotates, it turns two rollers. One roller is turned by side-to-side movement and the other by up-and-down movement.

2. Each roller turns a wheel with a pattern of slots cut into it.

3. Two special lamps, called *light emitting diodes* or LEDs, are attached to each roller. They send beams of light toward each wheel.

Ball

Roller

Wheel

LED

Detector

4. As the wheel turns, the slots interrupt the beam of light. Light-sensitive devices behind the wheel detect these changes and send this information to the computer.

Scanners

Scanners are the eyes of your computer. They can "see" images or printed text and translate them into binary code.

Most scanners collect data from a page by recording which areas are light and which are dark. They contain a camera which is made up of thousands of tiny cells, called charge-coupled devices (CCDs). Each CCD detects whether a small part of the image is either light or dark. It transmits this data to the CPU, which then creates the image. Some scanners are sensitive enough to tell the difference between colors.

Most scanners have 90,000 CCDs per square inch (over 35,000 in a cm²). It would take more than 3000 CCDs to scan an image the size of a pinhead!

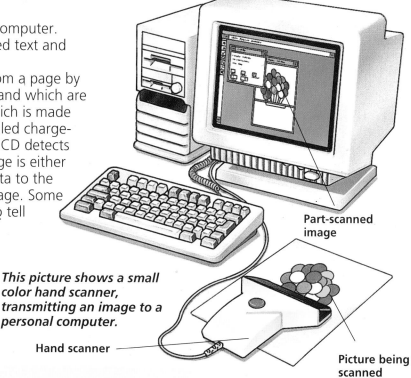

Part-scanned image

This picture shows a small color hand scanner, transmitting an image to a personal computer.

Hand scanner

Picture being scanned

Reading text

Computers can be used to "read" text or symbols on a printed page. For example, a computer can mark multiple choice exams by registering where x's have been put on the page.

Optical character readers (**OCRs**) work by scanning each letter on a page and then comparing it with characters stored in the computer's memory.

This is called **matrix matching**. OCRs can read a huge variety of different styles of lettering.

Another type of OCR instructs the computer to copy the shapes it finds on a page. This is called **feature analysis**.

All OCRs make mistakes. For example, the word "clown" can be misread as the word "down".

An OCR feature analysis scan of the letter "R"

Computer's match

Original letter

Touchscreens

A touchscreen has a built-in system of wires which are sensitive to the touch of a finger. You can select options and give commands by pressing different areas on the screen.

A touchscreen at the EPCOT Center, in Walt Disney World, Florida, lets visitors find out about the different rides.

Output hardware

The information that a computer produces is called **output**. In the computer, output is in the form of binary code. **Output hardware**, such as monitors and printers, decodes binary code and puts it into a form that you can understand.

Output can be displayed on a screen, or printed on paper or film (see page 25). Printed output is called **hard copy**. Output on screen is called **soft copy**.

Cathode ray monitors

A monitor displays computer data on a screen. The most common monitors work in the same way as televisions. Electrical signals are converted into an image on the screen by a device called a **cathode ray tube** (**CRT**).

A CRT contains a gun that fires a beam of electrons (electrical particles) at the screen. This diagram shows how these beams are converted into color graphics.

1. The CPU sends electrical pulses (which represent a picture) to an adaptor. This converts pulses into three beams of electrons, representing blue, green and red.

ADAPTOR

Electron beams

Shadow mask

2. Electron beams pass through holes in a metal plate called a shadow mask. The mask keeps beams on target, so they hit the screen where they are meant to.

3. Electrons strike a dot, called a pixel, on inside of the screen.

Pixel

Red

Blue   Green

4. Each pixel is made up of three spots of chemicals which glow when hit by electrons. The three spots glow different colors: red, blue and green.

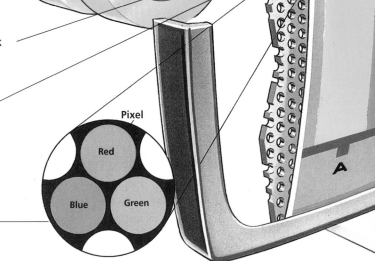

5. The stronger the electron beam, the stronger color the chemical gives out. To make different colors, the strength of each beam is varied. So strong red, strong blue and weak green beams will make purple, but strong green, strong red and weak blue beams will make brown.

6. Only one pixel is lit up at a time. But the beam of electrons sweeps so quickly over screen that you see a complete picture.

Monochrome monitors

A few computers still have monochrome monitors. This means that they use just one color plus black. *(Mono* means "one" and *chrome* means "color".) Three common examples are green, white or orange text on a black background. But, like TVs, nearly all new monitors are color.

Green text on a black background

White text on a black background

Orange text on a black background

Flat screen monitors

CRT monitors are too bulky for portable computers. Instead they have **flat screen monitors.** Many of these use **liquid crystal display** (**LCD**) screens. An LCD screen is filled with molecules (tiny particles) of a liquid which reflects the light. When the screen is scanned by the computer, some molecules "twist" to shut out the light. The "off" molecules cause a pixel to turn dark, and so form part of the image.

An LCD screen

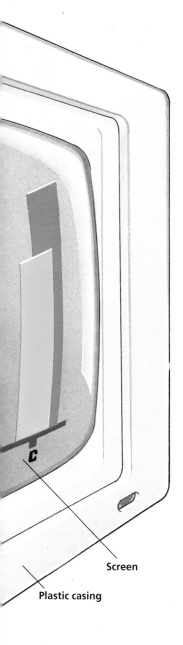

C

Screen

Plastic casing

Sound

Using a **sound synthesizer,** computers can produce output in the form of sound. All sound is produced by vibrations in the air, called sound waves. In a sound synthesizer, electrical signals are converted into sound waves by a device, called an **oscillator.** Sound software is used to mix musical sounds, and create new sounds. Some sound software can create waves that are similar to those of human speech. This is called **speech synthesis.** Some telephone inquiry services use speech synthesis.

645
73832

Printers

In the early days of computers, many people thought that working with paper would soon be a thing of the past, as all information would be kept on disks. But this hasn't happened. Computers can go wrong and disks can become "corrupt" so they can no longer be read. One way to make sure you don't lose any data is to make print-outs. Some different types of printers are described here.

Dot matrix printers

Dot matrix printers are made up of steel pins which strike a piece of paper through an inked ribbon to create a pattern of tiny dots or squares. The dots, or squares, appear to join up to print graphics or text. How well the print comes out depends on the number of steel pins in the machine. A 350 dpi (dots per inch) machine will produce better quality print than a 150 dpi (dots per inch) machine.

A dot matrix printer

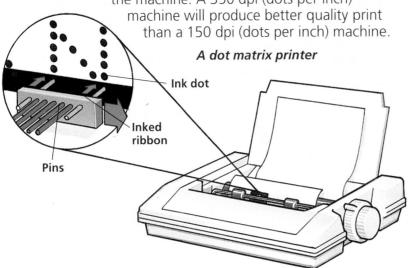

Ink dot

Inked ribbon

Pins

Ink jet printers

Inkjet printers print pictures or characters using fine jets of ink which are squirted out of tiny nozzles onto paper. The ink is kept in reservoirs and fed into 50 firing chambers just below each nozzle. Some printers have four colors of inks - so hundreds of different colors can be created by mixing them together.

How an inkjet printer works

Firing chamber

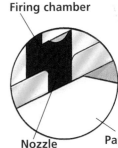

An electric current flows along bottom of firing chamber. This makes ink boil and a bubble of steam forms.

Nozzle   Paper

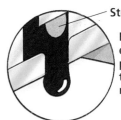

Steam bubble

Bubble expands and pushes ink through nozzle.

The pressure of steam bubble forces a droplet of ink to be squirted out onto paper.

Daisy wheel printers

Daisy wheel printers have raised letters and numbers arranged on a wheel that looks like a daisy. The daisy wheel turns around until the correct letter is in position for a hammer to strike it against an inked ribbon.

A daisy wheel

"Petal" is struck.

Raised "D"

Inked ribbon

Printed "D"

Paper

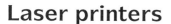

Laser printers

Laser printers use a beam of intense light (a laser beam) to convert binary data into print. They are very quick as they can print a whole page at once.

How a laser printer works

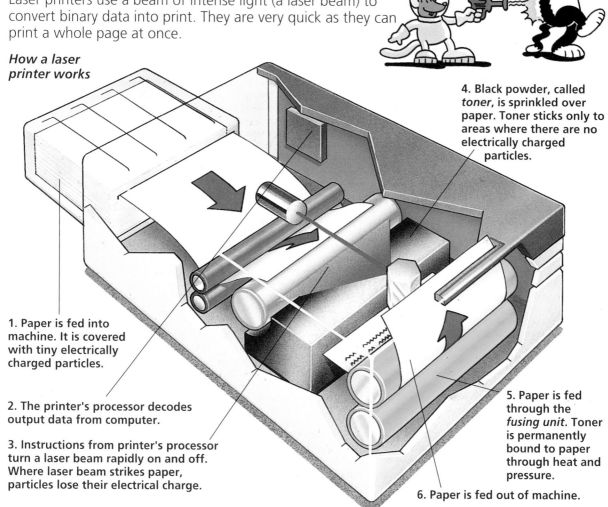

1. Paper is fed into machine. It is covered with tiny electrically charged particles.

2. The printer's processor decodes output data from computer.

3. Instructions from printer's processor turn a laser beam rapidly on and off. Where laser beam strikes paper, particles lose their electrical charge.

4. Black powder, called *toner*, is sprinkled over paper. Toner sticks only to areas where there are no electrically charged particles.

5. Paper is fed through the *fusing unit*. Toner is permanently bound to paper through heat and pressure.

6. Paper is fed out of machine.

Printer driver

A computer needs a piece of software called a **printer driver** in its CPU to help control the printer. The printer driver adapts output data so that a particular printer can understand it.

Print spooler

Often a computer can process data faster than its printer can print it. This can mean that the computer is held back from doing other jobs while it waits for the printer to catch up. A **print spooler** holds data while it is being fed to the printer. This leaves the computer free to do other work.

Mainframes

Mainframes are the largest, fastest and most expensive computers. They can process many millions of instructions per second. Over one hundred people can use a mainframe at the same time.

Each user has a **computer terminal**, which consists of a screen and a keyboard. Each terminal is linked to a CPU, where all the computer's calculations take place. Other hardware, such as printers, is linked to the mainframe too, and the whole system can take up as much room as a large house.

Running a mainframe

Mainframe systems are so large that they need many people to look after them. These people work in a **data processing (DP) department**.

The DP department shown in this diagram has four different sections: the operations section, the programming section, the systems analysis section and the information section.

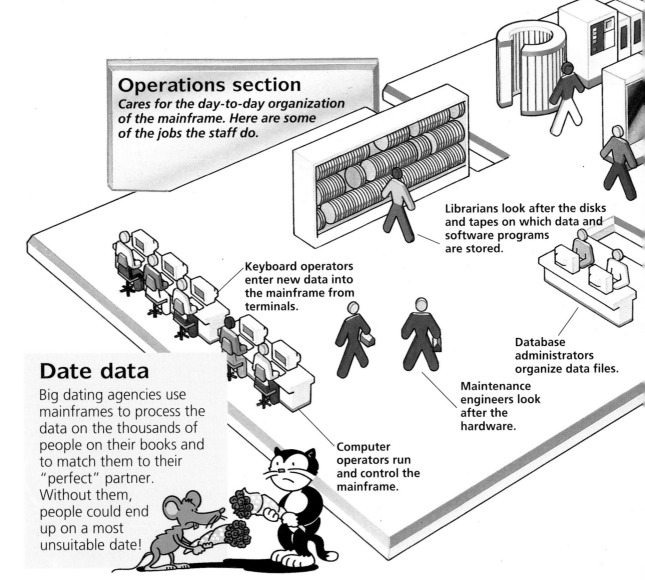

Operations section
Cares for the day-to-day organization of the mainframe. Here are some of the jobs the staff do.

Librarians look after the disks and tapes on which data and software programs are stored.

Keyboard operators enter new data into the mainframe from terminals.

Database administrators organize data files.

Maintenance engineers look after the hardware.

Computer operators run and control the mainframe.

Date data

Big dating agencies use mainframes to process the data on the thousands of people on their books and to match them to their "perfect" partner. Without them, people could end up on a most unsuitable date!

Open sesame

Mainframe users often have to type in a password before they can start work on their terminal. This stops outsiders from finding out confidential information. What password would you choose?

Programming section

Programmers develop new applications software.

Systems analysis section

Systems analysts design new computer systems to perform certain tasks. For example, a systems analyst will choose the best kind of computer software to suit a particular user's needs.

Information section

Users come here if, for example, their terminal breaks down or they need help with software.

Monsters

The biggest and fastest mainframes of all are called supercomputers, or "monsters". It takes a monster 90 seconds to do the work which a fast PC could complete in 20 hours. They are used for projects, such as weather predictions, which use masses of data.

Computers on the job

Computers have revolutionized everyone's lives. They have changed the way people work, play, shop and learn. Some jobs have been completely taken over by computers. Here are just some of the ways in which computers work for us and with us.

Milking the system

Farmers may soon be able to sleep later in the mornings, while robots milk their cows. Scientists have developed a milking system which can work without the farmer.

Robotic arm

2. Computer checks its memory to see when cow was last milked. If cow needs milking, computer uses a robotic arm to find udder and teats.

3. As robot milks cow, a computerized trough at the other end gives it food to keep it quiet.

4. If cow has returned to stall too soon, computer will open gate and cow will wander out.

1. Each cow is fitted with a small electronic tag. When a cow wanders into a milking stall, it is identified by a computer which reads its tag.

Medicine

Doctors use computers in hundreds of different ways. From simple software packages which help diagnose diseases, to complex machines that can scan the human brain, computers are now a vital part of modern medicine.

Computers monitor important data about patients' health. They can also control the amount of any drugs released into the bloodstream.

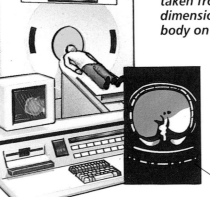

CAT scanners combine a series of X-rays taken from different angles to create a 3-dimensional image of part of the human body on a computer screen.

X-ray source moves around.

Scanner beam

Detector

One scan of a cross-section of a human kidney

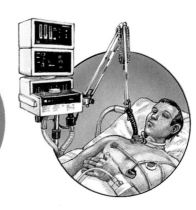

Bar codes

In most supermarkets, each item has a bar code - a label made up of columns of black lines. At the check-out, the bar code is passed over a bar code reader. A computer linked to this machine checks the bar code against a price list and sends the result back to the cash register.

This saves a lot of time. Each price does not have to be keyed into the cash register and price tags don't have to be put on each item. The diagram below shows how bar codes are read.

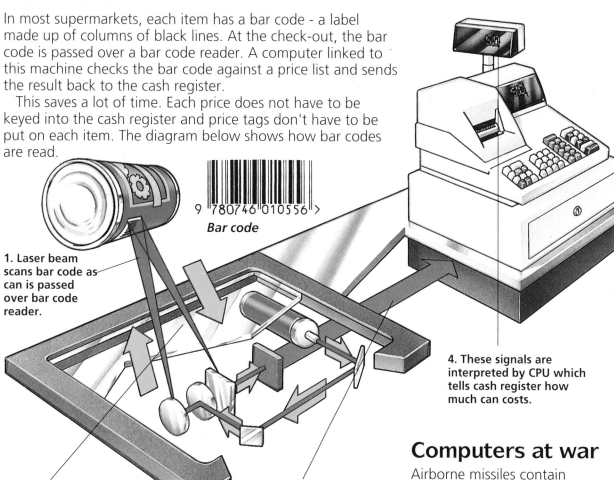

Bar code

1. Laser beam scans bar code as can is passed over bar code reader.

2. Beam is reflected back from bar code into a scanner.

3. Pattern of light and dark from bar code is changed into electronic signals. These are sent to a personal computer.

4. These signals are interpreted by CPU which tells cash register how much can costs.

Computers at war

Airborne missiles contain computers which guide them to their targets. They are loaded with electronic maps and can process information from satellites. This tells them where they are and where to go. These weapons are so accurate that they can be guided over long distances.

A Trident missile launched from a submarine.

Ringing the changes

The French telephone company, France Telecom, uses a computerized "phone book" called *Minitel*. Over 6.4 million homes all over France have small terminals which are linked up to a mainframe holding a database of phone numbers. The terminals can also link up to other mainframes, so people can use them to book train tickets or to call up the weather forecast.

Creative computers

Computers aren't just for figuring out calculations and analyzing data. They are also creative tools used by designers and artists.

Computer-aided design

Computer-aided design (CAD) software can be used to design anything from spoons to sports cars. If you enter a series of measurements into the computer, it will produce a 3-D image of the object on screen. This is not much quicker than drawing, but you can move the image around, view it from any angle, and make as many different versions as you want, without having to draw it from scratch each time.

CAD software can also check that a design "works". For example, the design of a plane can be tested for safety. By entering data about what the plane is made of and the pressure put on it in a hurricane, the program will predict if it can survive high winds.

The structure of a high-speed jet plane is first designed as a wire frame.

Designers can fill in the wire frame to see what the plane will actually look like.

Paintings and patterns

Painting software allows artists to create original pictures on a screen. With some packages you can draw freehand with a special pen on a special board. The lines you paint appear on screen.

Mathematicians have created some fantastical patterns, called **fractals**, on computers. They are based on mathematical formulas. Each part of the pattern has the same structure as the whole thing.

A fractal design created by feeding a series of numbers into a computer

A human face created by an artist using computer graphics

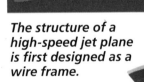

Desktop publishing

Desktop publishing (DTP) is the process by which words and pictures are put together on a computer to create publications, such as magazines.

DTP packages allow people to type text onto the screen, scan in the images which go with that text, and fit the words around the pictures. A DTP system can produce text in different styles of lettering, called **fonts**, and in different sizes. Designers can try out different fonts and different designs to see which one looks and fits the best.

Then and now

Today, most newspapers, magazines and books (including this one) are created with DTP, because it is quicker and cheaper than older ways. This diagram shows how one page of a publication was produced before DTP was available, and compares it with modern methods.

THEN

1. Text typed into a typewriter or word processor.

2. Text typed into a *typesetting* machine. This sets text in columns according to size and layout of page, and puts it in right font.

3. Text checked for errors and sent back to typesetting machine for corrections.

4. Text is pasted down in correct position, leaving spaces for pictures. Often text has to be cut or added to until it fits. Each time this happens, text has to go back to stage 1.

5. Pasted-up page sent to printers, where pictures are inserted.

6. Page transferred onto a sheet of clear plastic called *film*. Film is used to make plates, from which page is printed.

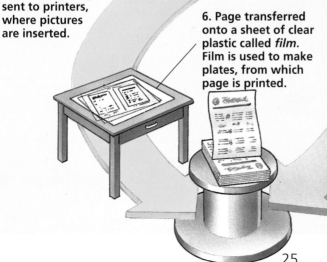

NOW

1. Text is typed straight onto screen in position, using right font.

2. Pictures are scanned onto page. Text and graphics can be adjusted on screen until they all fit together.

3. When page is ready, the text and pictures are printed out on film. This is sent to printers.

Communicating computers

Computers can be linked together so they can swap information and share equipment. Two or more computers that are joined in this way form a **computer network**.

Computers which can be linked together are said to be **compatible**. The link can be as simple as a telephone line, or as sophisticated as a satellite.

There are two main kinds of networks: local area networks and wide area networks. They are described on these pages.

Local area networks

Local area networks (LANs) link together computers in a small area, such as a building. They are very useful for teamwork when people need to know what each other is doing. Without LANs, people would constantly have to print out hard copy or exchange floppy disks. Using a LAN, data can be sent electronically between computers.

Electronic mail

Electronic mail, or e-mail, is one of the big benefits of a network. Using e-mail, a personal computer user can send documents or graphics to other personal computer users. All the sender has to do is type in the names of the people she wants to receive the document and press a key. Receivers who are working on their computers will see a message flash up on their screen saying "mail is waiting". They can read it and reply immediately.

Sendin electronic mail

**Person 1
Types in and sends a message.**

**Person 2
Reads message immediately on her monitor.**

**Person 3
(away from terminal) - Message flashes when terminal is turned on.**

File servers

Some linked PCs operate a **file server**. This is a hard disk shared by everyone on the LAN.

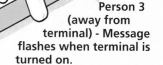

Wide area networks

Places that used to be cut off from the rest of the planet can now, with only electricity, a telephone and a computer terminal, be part of a worldwide network of computers. Computers all over the world can be linked as part of **wide area networks (WANs)**.

The network of cash dispensing machines, or automated teller machines (ATMs), is one of the widest networks. It links together thousands of bank computers across the globe. This means that an American on vacation in Europe can withdraw cash from a cash dispensing machine in France using an American withdrawal card.

This diagram shows how an ATM works.

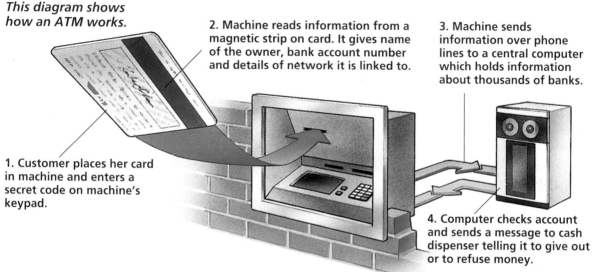

2. Machine reads information from a magnetic strip on card. It gives name of the owner, bank account number and details of network it is linked to.

3. Machine sends information over phone lines to a central computer which holds information about thousands of banks.

1. Customer places her card in machine and enters a secret code on machine's keypad.

4. Computer checks account and sends a message to cash dispenser telling it to give out or to refuse money.

Modems

Computers may need to use a device called a **modem** to communicate with each other via telephone lines. Some telephone systems send data in the form of waves, and not in pulses like a computer. A modem converts the pulses into waves so the telephone can understand them. At the receiving end, the modem converts waves back to pulses.

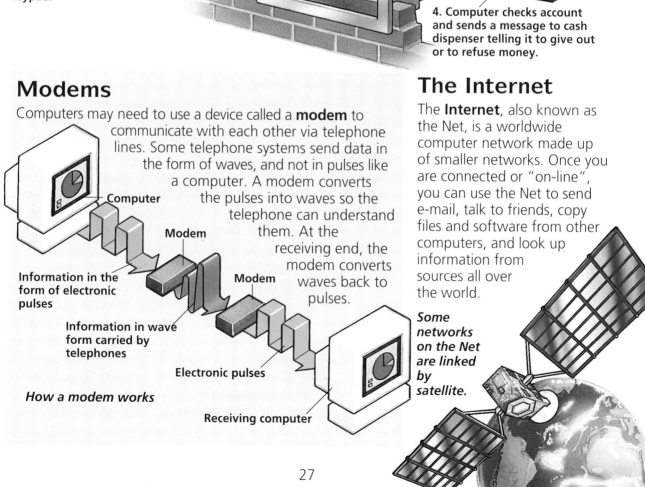

Computer

Modem

Modem

Information in the form of electronic pulses

Information in wave form carried by telephones

Electronic pulses

Receiving computer

How a modem works

The Internet

The **Internet**, also known as the Net, is a worldwide computer network made up of smaller networks. Once you are connected or "on-line", you can use the Net to send e-mail, talk to friends, copy files and software from other computers, and look up information from sources all over the world.

Some networks on the Net are linked by satellite.

Compact discs

The most common way of storing data on a portable disk is to store it on a compact disc or CD. CDs can store an amazing amount of data in the form of words, music, animated cartoons and pictures.

How much can a CD store?

 600 copies of the Bible

 72 minutes of cartoon or video

 2 hours of music

19 hours of speech

Data is written onto a CD by a strong laser beam which burns tiny pits into its surface. A **pit** stands for binary 1 and the absence of a pit, called a **land**, stands for binary 0. The disc is read by a weaker beam which passes over the surface of the disc as it turns.

How a CD is read

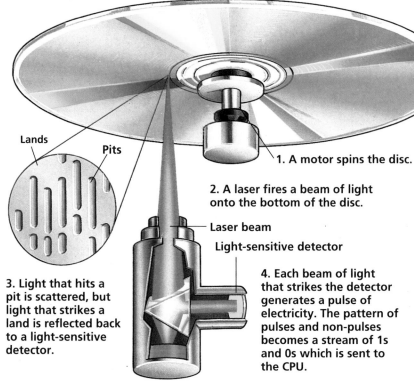

Lands

Pits

1. A motor spins the disc.

2. A laser fires a beam of light onto the bottom of the disc.

Laser beam

Light-sensitive detector

3. Light that hits a pit is scattered, but light that strikes a land is reflected back to a light-sensitive detector.

4. Each beam of light that strikes the detector generates a pulse of electricity. The pattern of pulses and non-pulses becomes a stream of 1s and 0s which is sent to the CPU.

Personal computers can be equipped with CD drives and speakers. There are three different types of compact discs which are described below.

Read-only optical discs

Read-only optical discs cannot be written on by the user. They can only be read. Data is encoded onto them when they are made and you cannot wipe it off or change it. The most popular read-only optical discs come as compact discs and are known as CD-ROMs.

WORMs

Write-once, read-many optical discs (WORMs) are blank CDs on which you can write your own data. But only once. After you have stored the data you can read it from the disc, but you cannot change it or wipe it off.

Erasable optical discs

Erasable optical discs can store as much as other CDs but, like magnetic disks, you can wipe them clean and use them again. They are probably the discs of the future. You can't buy them in all shops yet, because more research is needed to make them cheaper.

Multimedia presentations

Multimedia means using computers to combine text, sound, graphics and video. **Multimedia presentations** are combinations of sound, text, still pictures and videos that are usually stored on a CD. You can also see them on the Net. Most multi-media presentations are **interactive**. This means you can take part in or control the program.

These are some of the things you can do with a CD-ROM about wildlife.

Find out about different species.

Study the vivid patterns and shapes of butterflies.

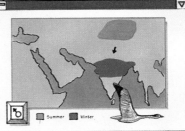

Chart the migration routes of geese.

Hear the cry of a toucan.

Learn how to help endangered species.

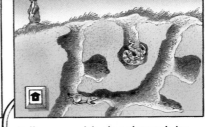

Follow a prairie dog through its maze-like burrow.

You work your way through the "pages" using your mouse to choose different options.

You can also buy CD-ROM stories in which you become one of the characters. You can find yourself trapped in a haunted house, investigating a murder or embarking on an around-the-world journey, and it's up to you to make it a happy ending.

Fitting it in

Pictures take up lots of room on a CD, so a process called **data compression** is used to save space. Much of the data in a picture is the same. For example, large areas of sky may be the same blue. Using data compression, only one tiny dot of blue is recorded on disc. When the image is created on screen, an instruction is given to copy that dot in all the sky areas.

Virtual reality

Computer technology can create worlds that don't exist and make you believe you can see, hear and touch them. This is called **virtual reality**. When you watch TV, it's as if you were looking through a window, but with virtual reality you actually feel you are part of the picture itself.

Headsets

In order to experience virtual reality you may have to wear a headset with two screens in front of each eye. 3-D scenes are projected onto these screens. Some headsets contain earphones with stereo sound as well.

Sensors in the headset pick up your head movements and convert this information into signals which are sent to a computer. The computer responds by changing the image on the screens as you move your head.

Data gloves

Data gloves contain sensors which detect the movements of your hand. If, for example, you were looking at the image of a room, you could stretch out and open a door. The graphics would change to show the door opening and pressure pads in the gloves would press down on your hand, so you would also <u>feel</u> as if you were turning a door handle.

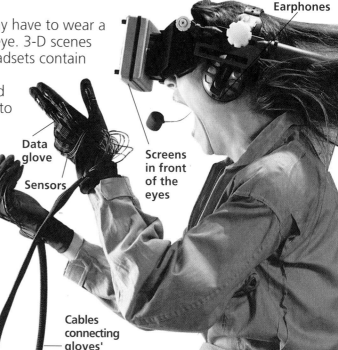

Virtual reality headset

Earphones

Data glove

Sensors

Screens in front of the eyes

Cables connecting gloves' sensors to computer

Flight simulator

A flying start

Flight simulators are virtual reality systems used for training pilots. A trainee sits in a "cockpit" and a virtual reality scene is projected onto the windshield. The controls inside the cockpit are linked to a computer which alters the view and tilts and turns the cockpit as the trainee tries to "fly". It is so realistic that it feels as if you are in a real plane.

View from inside the Concept 90 flight simulator

Robodoc

A virtual reality system is being developed which allows a surgeon in one part of the world to operate on a patient thousands of miles away. The surgeon is transmitted a life-size video display of the patient, via satellite. He holds hand-controllers that give him an impression of what the patient's body feels like. The surgeon can then perform the operation using the hand controls. His movements are sent back to the operating room. There a robot is programmed to follow the surgeon's hand movements exactly.

Robodoc at work

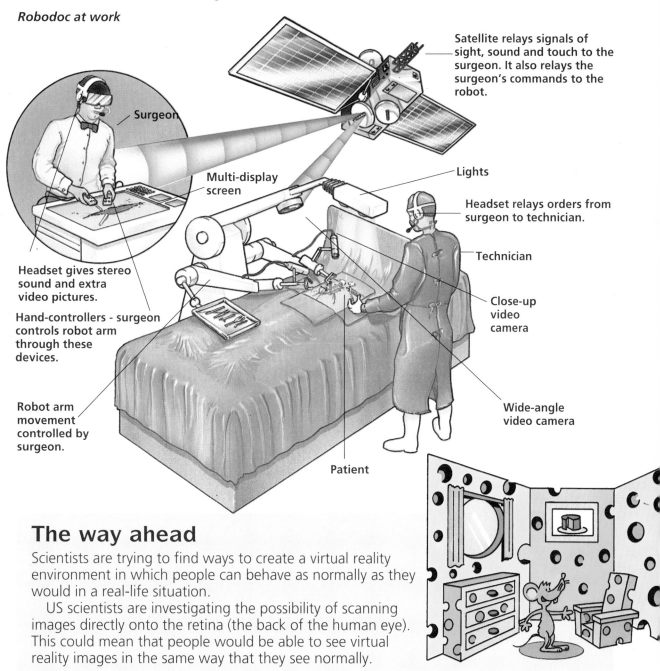

Surgeon

Satellite relays signals of sight, sound and touch to the surgeon. It also relays the surgeon's commands to the robot.

Multi-display screen

Lights

Headset relays orders from surgeon to technician.

Technician

Headset gives stereo sound and extra video pictures.

Hand-controllers - surgeon controls robot arm through these devices.

Close-up video camera

Robot arm movement controlled by surgeon.

Wide-angle video camera

Patient

The way ahead

Scientists are trying to find ways to create a virtual reality environment in which people can behave as normally as they would in a real-life situation.

US scientists are investigating the possibility of scanning images directly onto the retina (the back of the human eye). This could mean that people would be able to see virtual reality images in the same way that they see normally.

Computer crime

The Maltese Amoeba may sound like a funny cartoon character, but if it attacked your computer you wouldn't be laughing. The Maltese Amoeba is a computer virus. It is a form of software which can "infect" your system and destroy your data.

Making computer viruses is only one type of computer crime. Others include hacking (changing data in a computer without permission) and pirating (illegally copying software programs).

Viruses

Viruses are programs which are written deliberately to damage data. Viruses can hide themselves in a computer system. Some viruses are fairly harmless. Others have more serious effects. They can wipe out all your data or turn it into gobbledegook.

Once a virus is in your computer it can infect your disks. If you then lend them to someone or if your computer is part of a

network, the virus will spread. The best way to combat a virus is with anti-virus software, which makes computers safe from many types of viruses.

Michelangelo virus

The Michelangelo virus was programmed to become active on March 6, 1992, the 517th birthday of the Italian painter Michelangelo. It attacked computer systems throughout the world, turning data on hard disks into nonsense.

Gulf virus

A US magazine claimed that a computer virus was used by the US against Iraq during the Gulf War in 1992. It suggested that US spies had put an infected chip into a printer the Iraqis had bought. The chip was designed to muddle the mainframe computer in Iraq's military control center.

Cascade virus

When the Cascade virus attacks, all the letters in a file fall into a heap at the bottom of the screen. This looks spectacular but it's hard to see the funny side when it's your document.

Hacked off

Criminals who get into computer systems without permission are called **hackers**. Using telephone lines, hackers link up their own computers to networks, so they can call up private files. By changing information in the files, they can steal money and goods without being caught. For example, a file may record that 10 bicycles were sold on Tuesday. By changing it to 11, the hacker can steal one and no one will know it is missing.

Modern espionage relies heavily on hacking, because top secret government records are often kept on computer. It's more important for today's spy to be a master of mainframes than to be a master of disguises.

Governments often scramble secret information in a computer, so even if someone could hack into it they wouldn't be able to read it. Modern computers can develop incredibly complex codes which would take a human years to unscramble. The data can only be read using a special decoding program.

Programs and languages

Programs (the sets of commands) given to a computer have to be carefully written. Otherwise mistakes, known as bugs, can stop the computer from carrying out its job properly. It is important to remember that computers can only follow the instructions they are given. They cannot "see what you mean" or "get the hang of it" as they go along.

Here is a list of instructions for a door-to-door charity collection, written as if it were a program for a robot. Although a human being *would have no problem following them, they contain a bug which would leave a computer unable to do the task. Can you spot what it is?*

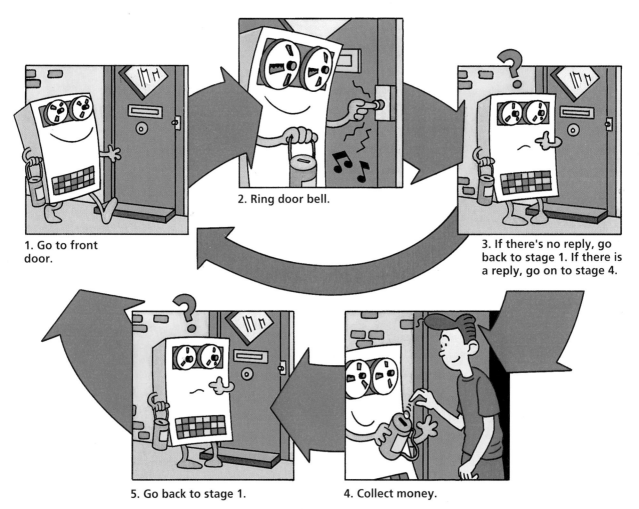

1. Go to front door.

2. Ring door bell.

3. If there's no reply, go back to stage 1. If there is a reply, go on to stage 4.

5. Go back to stage 1.

4. Collect money.

When commanded to go back to stage 1 at stages 3 or 5, the robot finds that it is at a front door already. So it will repeat the cycle, but at *the same house. This is obviously not what the programmer meant to happen. A better command would be: 1. Go to nearest unvisited front door.*

Computer-speak

Computers can only read instructions written in binary code. It is possible to write programs straight into binary, but it takes ages and needs seemingly endless rows of 0s and 1s.

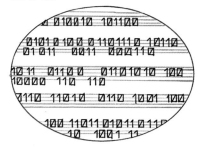

So **computer languages** have been developed that use decimal numbers, words and symbols instead. These are then converted by other programs into binary code.

There are two main types of programming languages: high-level and low-level languages.

High-level languages

High-level languages are the most common type of computer language. They are the easiest to learn because they use words similar to our own.

High-level languages are converted into binary code by using a program called an **interpreter,** or one called a **compiler**.

An interpreter works as a program is running. It takes one line of the program's

instructions at a time. It checks that the instruction is correct and then it carries it out.

A compiler works before a program is run. It translates all the instructions in the

program into binary code at once and then it carries them out.

Low-level languages

Low-level languages give a computer instructions in the form of abbreviations. For example, LD may be used for the command "load program", or JMP for "jump".

Computers need a program called an **assembler** to translate low-level languages into binary code. A **disassembler** converts binary back into the programming language.

An assembler converts "JMP" into binary.

A disassembler converts it back again.

Thinking machines?

Computers in storybooks and on TV have exciting personalities and can do everything humans can do and more. But in real life things aren't quite like that.

Some computers appear to have human powers of reasoning and logic. But machines can't really think in the way that people can. When a computer seems clever, it just means that the programmer was intelligent.

Things computers do that make them look intelligent:

Build cars.

Beat all but the very best players at chess.

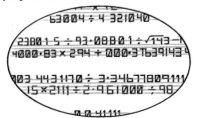

Figure out complicated problems involving hundreds of figures.

Dummies

Computers can only follow instructions. Most of the things that people do every day, even the ones that we think are really simple, are so complex that it would be impossible to explain them as a set of instructions. This means that computers cannot do them. This robot has been programmed to carry packages across a busy town. But the program just isn't good enough.

Robobike is programmed to do all these things:

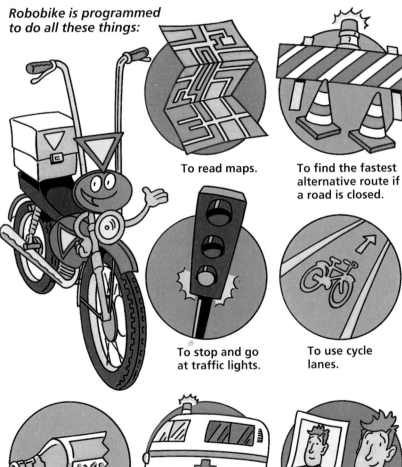

To read maps.

To find the fastest alternative route if a road is closed.

To stop and go at traffic lights.

To use cycle lanes.

To swerve around obstacles and broken glass.

To phone an ambulance if there's an accident.

To recognize the receiver of the package by matching his face with a pre-scanned photograph.

But, despite all these instructions, all sorts of things can, and do, go wrong.

On his way, robobike passes the filming of a car crash for a TV drama. The robot, not recognizing cameras, calls for an ambulance.

On arrival, the receiver tries to collect his parcel. Robobike won't release it. The receiver has grown a beard over the weekend and so he no longer matches the robot's photographic image.

On the way back, a traffic light gets stuck on red. The robot waits there for hours and eventually is run over by a truck.

Robobike has failed. A person could have coped with these new situations as they arose. But when it comes to making decisions in unexpected circumstances, computers are no good.

Working by the rules

Computers are only good at tasks which never vary and are identical every single time they are done. But when they are good, they are very, very good. They can be much quicker and much more reliable than human beings.

Mike works in a factory. His job is to put a cherry on the top of sweet rolls.

Some days, if he's watched too much TV, his eyes get a bit blurry and the cherry doesn't end up exactly in the middle.

On other days, his sweet tooth gets the better of him and some cherries never quite make it to the rolls.

And a lot of the time he daydreams about his summer vacation and forgets the cherries altogether.

The cherry-placing process is a repetitive task which can be done by following a set of instructions. This makes it ideal for a robot, which will never be tempted to eat the cherries or doze off. So it is because they can't think that machines are better at these jobs than people, not because they can.

All the jobs computers do well are ones that can be broken down into a limited number of rules and commands. Even chess, which we think of as a game for the brainy, is actually a game of rules, which a computer can be "taught".

The future

Will scientists ever be able to put enough rules into a computer so it can make decisions like a person? Some scientists think not. Others believe that, as more is understood about how the human brain works, scientists will be able to use this knowledge to make the first truly intelligent computers.

Computer firsts

Charles Babbage, a Scottish mathematician, is the "father" of the computer. Although other people had already invented mechanical calculating machines, he was the first to figure out how a machine could perform many different sorts of calculations and store the results.

Charles Babbage (1792-1871)

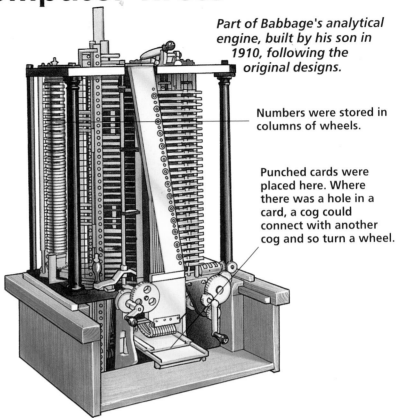

Part of Babbage's analytical engine, built by his son in 1910, following the original designs.

Numbers were stored in columns of wheels.

Punched cards were placed here. Where there was a hole in a card, a cog could connect with another cog and so turn a wheel.

In 1833, Babbage started designing his machine, which he called an "analytical engine". His engine followed the same principles as the modern computer - but instead of passing though logic gates (see page 4), coded data was to be fed through a series of cogs and wheels. A woman named Ada Lovelace worked with Babbage, making programs for the engine in the form of cards with holes punched in them.

Punched cards

Ada Lovelace (1815-1852)

Babbage devoted the last 37 years of his life to building his machine, but he died before he had completed it. In fact, even if he had lived until he was a hundred, it is unlikely that it would ever have been built. His engine was so complicated, with so many intricate moving parts, that the technology at the time would not have been up to it.

Numbers and pulses

By the 1930s, punched cards were widely used in calculators and simple computers. All these computers made calculations using the decimal system (the numbers 0-9). In 1941, a German engineer named Konrad Zuse made a computer that operated using binary code (the numbers 0-1).

In 1945, the first computer to code data as electrical pulses was built. These inventions marked the beginning of the age of modern computers.

Valves and transistors

One of the first and most famous electronic calculating machines was ENIAC (Electronic Numerical Integrator Analyzer and Computer). It was built for the US Army in 1945 by Presper Eckert and John Mauchly. Its equipment filled a large room. Data was processed through a series of large electronic switches called valves.

ENIAC, one of the world's first electronic computers

ENIAC weighed the same as 500 people and covered 74 square meters of floor space.

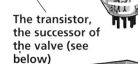

Valve

The transistor, the successor of the valve (see below)

P. Eckert and J. Mauchly with a part of ENIAC

Valves took up a lot of space, used a lot of power and got very hot. In 1953, devices called transistors were invented to replace them. Transistors were smaller, cheaper and used less power. This meant they could be packed closer together, so computers became smaller.

Did you know?

Babbage used the word computer to describe the people who performed calculations on his machines. The word was not used to mean the machines until the 20th century.

Then and now

William Shanks, a 19th century English teacher, took 28 years to figure out, to 707 decimal places, the value of a number used in geometry called π (said as pi). A modern computer program can calculate the answer in seven seconds. When the program was first used it revealed that Shanks had made an error in the 528th figure of his calculation.

Chip revolution

In the mid-1960s, the chip was developed (see page 4). Chips contain the equivalent of millions of transistors, all linked together to form a circuit. An electronic circuit the size of a postage stamp can do the work previously done by a large cabinet of transistors.

A silicon chip in its plastic casing

Computer health

If you don't take care, you can damage your health working on computers. Especially if you spend long stretches at the screen. But if you follow some simple guidelines you can enjoy a danger-free time.

Eyes

Most monitors have an anti-glare screen. But if yours doesn't, wear tinted glasses. You may feel a bit silly wearing sunglasses indoors, but it could stop you from getting headaches.

Eyes can become strained by focusing at the same distance for a long time. So, every ten minutes or so, look away from the screen and focus your eyes on something farther away.

Posture

Sitting at a computer can strain your shoulders and the bottom of your back, so it is important to sit in a good chair. Find one that can be adjusted to support your lower back and allows you to have both feet on the floor. Your elbows and knees should be bent at 90°. Sit directly in front of your monitor and keyboard. Your keyboard should be at the same height as your elbows.

Shrug your shoulders and shake your hands at regular intervals to relieve tension which builds up in your muscles and joints.

RSI

Doctors think that an illness called **repetitive strain syndrome** (**RSS**) can be caused by working at a keyboard and using a mouse every day. It mostly affects wrists, fingers and arms, and has symptoms similar to arthritis. It can be very painful and forces people to give up work. When typing, make sure your wrists are completely relaxed and flat, never bent.

This diagram shows the best way to sit at your computer.

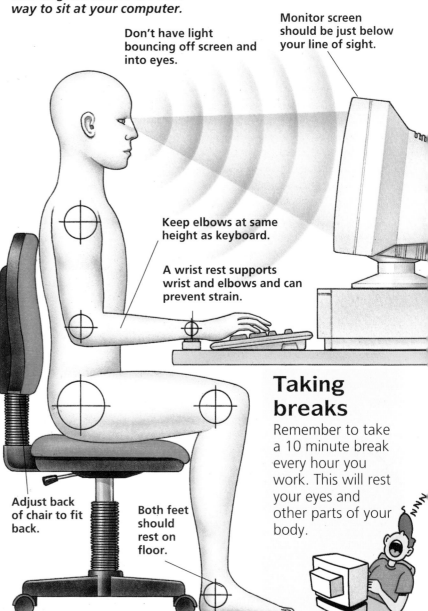

Don't have light bouncing off screen and into eyes.

Monitor screen should be just below your line of sight.

Keep elbows at same height as keyboard.

A wrist rest supports wrist and elbows and can prevent strain.

Adjust back of chair to fit back.

Both feet should rest on floor.

Taking breaks

Remember to take a 10 minute break every hour you work. This will rest your eyes and other parts of your body.

Looking after the hardware

Your computer needs looking after too. It will work much better and last much longer if it is taken care of properly. Here are some dos and don'ts of looking after hardware.

Do

Avoid smoke.
Avoid dust.

Avoid high temperatures and humidity.

Keep drinks and food away.

Use a special program to protect, or "park", the hard disk when moving the systems unit. Put a cardboard dummy floppy disk in the floppy disk drive.

Store your floppy disks carefully in a plastic box.

Don't

Don't turn your computer on and off many times throughout the day.

Don't leave the monitor on for long periods at a time with the same image on the screen. You can buy a piece of software, called a screen saver, which will blank out the screen if the computer has not been used for a certain length of time.

Don't let your computer share an electric socket with another large electrical appliance, such as a refrigerator.

Times of trouble

If your computer stops working, first check that all your cables are properly connected. It's embarrassing to call a technician only to find your dad had unplugged your machine to do the vacuuming.

Read your manual to make sure you're not doing anything wrong. You could try switching off and restarting the system. If this works, look out for the problem happening again and see if you can figure out what triggers the fault.

Most hardware and software manufacturers have a helpline you can call for advice. Remember, if you take your computer apart yourself, your guarantee may no longer be valid. So, don't attempt to fiddle with the electronics yourself.

If your manuals are too full of jargon to understand, you can buy simpler guides that explain things more clearly.

Organizing your files

Make sure that your files on the hard disk are organized into different directories so you can find them easily.

At the end of every day, always copy files from your hard disk onto two sets of floppy disks. Then if you lose any files from the hard disk, or if one set of floppy disks corrupts, you will still have a copy of your work. This is called **backing up**.

When you have backed up files that you are no longer working on, remove them from the hard disk. If the hard disk gets too full, data can become jumbled and your computer starts working more slowly.

Buying a personal computer

Here is a checklist of things to do and decisions to make before you choose any computer hardware or software.

Hardware checklist

Write a list of all the jobs you want your computer system to do.

Check that you like the layout of the keyboard.

Decide how much money you can afford to spend and stick to this limit.

Do you want to use your computer to explore the Internet or send e-mail (see pages 26 and 27)? If you do, you will need a modem.

Buy a computer with the largest hard disk you can afford, so that you have enough room to store all the programs you may want to use.

When choosing a printer, think about cost and speed; whether you want to print in color or monochrome, and the quality of the print. Ask to see samples of a printer's output.

If you want to use multimedia presentations (see page 29), you will need a CD drive. Most software is supplied on CD-ROM as well as disks. You will also need a soundcard and speakers to enjoy all the multimedia features.

Make sure you've got enough room for all the hardware you intend to buy.

Software checklist

Is the software you want to buy compatible with your hardware?

Talk to people who have used different brands of software, to see which packages they recommend. Read reviews of new software packages (and hardware) in computer magazines.

Software packages are revised and updated. You don't always need the most recent version. Older ones are cheaper and may provide all the features you need.

Do you want an integrated software package that combines certain features, such as word processing, database and spreadsheets? It may cost less than buying each application separately.

Some hardware manufacturers or suppliers give away software packages with their machines. Keep a lookout for the best deals and bargains.

Buying the computer

If you are buying your first computer, try to find someone who has experience with computers to help you.

Visit or telephone a variety of stores to find out their price for the computer system you want. Look at the prices in computer magazines.

Ask the salesman to demonstrate any hardware you are interested in. For example, when a monitor is demonstrated, check that the images are sharp in all areas of the screen.

You might consider buying a second-hand computer. But watch out for damage and test each part of the system thoroughly.

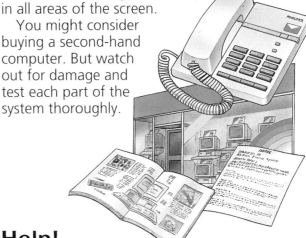

Help!

Most companies that supply hardware and software offer a support service to their customers. This includes help and advice on how to get the most out of your equipment and what to do if something goes wrong.

Try to buy hardware and software that come with a telephone support service that answers any questions and helps with problems. Many software packages come with a free training program.

Make sure your hardware comes with a guarantee. This is a promise by the manufacturer to repair your equipment free of charge for a certain period of time. Make sure your equipment is guaranteed for at least a year. Ideally, choose a company that promises to repair your equipment at home.

Computer words

The list below defines some of the more difficult computer words in this book. It also explains other technical terms you may come across when reading and talking about computers. When a definition contains a word that is explained elsewhere in this list, the word appears in *italics*.

Address. A number given to a specific location in a computer's *memory* where *data* is stored.

Applications software. *Programs* which enable a computer to carry out a particular task, such as *word processing* or calculations.

Arithmetic unit. The part of the computer's *CPU* that processes *data*, carrying out all the operations and calculations.

Assembler. A *program* that translates a *low-level language* into *machine code*.

Backup. A copy of *software* or *data* stored on disks or tape.

Binary code. A method of counting using just two digits, 0 and 1.

Booting up. The process in which *ROM* sends instructions to the *CPU* to start operations when a computer is turned on.

Bug. An error in *a program* which prevents a computer from carrying out its task.

Bus. A metal pathway connecting one part of a computer to another along which *data* flows in the form of *electronic* pulses.

Byte. Eight *bits*.

Cathode ray tube (**CRT**). A device which creates an image on a screen using a beam of *electrons* which scans the surface of the screen.

Central Processing Unit (**CPU**). The part of a computer that contains the *control unit* and the *arithmetic unit*. The CPU carries out the instructions of a *program*. Sometimes the term CPU includes *RAM*.

Chip. A tiny slice of *silicon* covered with millions of *electronic circuits* and *logic gates*.

Compact disc (CD). An *optical disc*, 4¾ inches wide.

Compiler. A *program* which translates instructions written in a *high-level language* into *machine code*.

Control unit. Part of the *CPU* that controls the movement of *data* between the *memory*, *arithmetic unit* and other *peripherals* when it is following programs.

CPU. See *Central Processing Unit*.

Cursor. A flashing symbol or pointer on a screen that shows the user where the next character or number will appear.

Data. The name given to all the information (numbers, characters, symbols and *graphics*) processed and produced by a computer.

Database. A collection of information stored in *files* that can be found easily.

Data compression. A way of reducing the amount of *data* that has to be stored or transmitted. It is often used for *graphics*.

Decimal code. A counting system that uses the digits 0-9.

Decryption. A method of making sense of *data* which has been scrambled by *encryption*.

Desktop publishing (**DTP**). A system of producing publications (books, magazines, newspapers, etc.) on a *personal computer* using special *software*.

Digital processing. The processing of *data* in binary 0s and 1s.

Disassembler. A *program* that converts *machine code* back into the assembler language.

Disk. A round piece of metal or plastic covered in magnetic material on which *data* is stored.

Disk drive. A device that *reads from* or *writes to* a *disk*.

Diskette. See *floppy disk*

Electronic. Concerned with, or using, devices that work by electricity.

E-mail (**Electronic mail**). A method of sending messages between computers in a *network*.

Encryption. A method of scrambling *data* for security reasons, so it cannot be understood without a *decryption* program.

Expansion slot. A slot in a *motherboard* to which extra *PCBs* can be added.

File. A collection of *data* stored as one unit - often called a document.

Floppy disk. A small, flexible *disk* used for storing *data*.

Format. To prepare a *disk* so that information can be *read from* or *written to* it.

Function keys. Keys on a keyboard that have special jobs and are usually labelled F1, F2, etc.

Gigabyte. 1024 *megabytes*.

Graphics. The information displayed on a screen or on a print-out in the form of diagrams, pictures, graphs and symbols.

GUI (Graphical User Interface). A system that uses on-screen pictures which can be clicked on with a mouse to give a computer instructions.

Hacker. A person who gains access to a computer system illegally.

Hard copy. Printed computer *output*, usually on paper.

Hard disk. A *disk* that remains permanently inside a *systems unit*, on which *data* is stored. The hard disks of some laptop and *notebook* computers can be removed and locked away to keep data safe.

Hardware. Computer equipment that you can touch.

High-level language. A computer language that is written like everyday language.

Icon. A picture you can click on to make your computer do something, or which appears to indicate that your computer is doing something.

Information. The term sometimes used for *data* that has been processed into a form that is useful to the user.

Information technology (IT). The processing, storage, and communication of information using computers and *electronics*.

Input. *Data* that goes into a computer.

Integrated circuit. A collection of *transistors* and *electronic circuits* built onto a piece of material called silicon. It is also called a *chip*.

Interface.The *hardware* or *software* which links two different parts of a computer and allows them to work together.

Internet (or the **Net**). A computer *network* made up of millions of linked computers.

Interpreter. A *program* that translates a *high-level language* into *machine code*, line by line.

ISDN (Integrated Services Digital Network). A type of high speed telephone line which can transmit *data* between computers very quickly.

Kilobyte (Kb). 1,024 *bytes*.

Laser printer. A *printer* that creates an image made up of tiny dots using a laser beam.

Light pen. An *input* device that can be used to draw images or point to things on a screen.

Local area network (LAN). Computers linked together over a small area, such as an office.

Logic gates. Tiny *electronic* devices which can change electronic pulses to non-pulses. They perform all the operations inside an *arithmetic unit*.

Low-level language. A computer language that uses codes similar to *machine code*.

Machine code. The language a computer uses to carry out tasks. It is based on *binary code*.

Mainframe. A large computer with lots of users. It has massive storage and high processing speeds.

Megabyte (Mb). 1,048,576 *bytes*.

Memory. The part of a computer that stores *data* and *program* instructions.

Minicomputer. A small

mainframe computer.

MIPS (Million instructions per second). The unit used to measure the speed at which a computer processes information.

Modem. A device which converts computer *data* so it can be carried down a telephone line.

Monitor. A device, which usually uses a *CRT*, that displays information on a screen.

Motherboard. The main *printed circuit board* inside a computer's *systems unit*.

Mouse. An *input* device used to move a pointer on a screen.

Network. A number of computers linked together so they can swap *data* and share *hardware*.

Notebook. A small battery-operated *personal computer*.

Operating system. *Software* that manages the overall operation of a computer system.

Optical disc. A *disc* that can be *read from* and *written to* with a laser beam. It is used for storing *data*.

Output. The results of computer processing, usually displayed on a screen or printed onto paper.

PDAs. Tiny computers that can fit on the palm of a hand.

Peripheral. Any *hardware* device that is controlled by a computer. For example, a *mouse*, a *keyboard* and a printer.

Personal computer (PC). A small computer operated by one user at a time.

Pixels (short for picture elements). The dots out of which images on a computer screen are built up.

Printed circuit board (PCB). A board on which the *electronic* devices in a computer are mounted. Metal strips connect one device with another.

Program. A set of instructions given to a computer that tells it how to do a particular job.

Random-access memory (RAM). The temporary *memory* where *data* and *programs* are stored while a

computer is using them.

Read-only memory (ROM). A permanent *memory* that stores *data* even when a computer is turned off.

Read from. To take *data* from a storage device, such as a *floppy disk,* and load it into *RAM*.

Resolution. A measurement of how sharp the image is on a screen. High resolutions screens are better quality than low resolution ones.

Saving. The process of storing *data* from RAM on a *disk*.

Scanner. A device that can convert an image into *binary code,* so it can be displayed on a screen.

Silicon. An element found in sand and quartz. It is used to make *chips*.

Silicon chip. See *chip*.

Software. All the *programs* and *data* that can be run on a computer.

Spreadsheet. A *program* that performs calculations on *data* arranged in rows and columns.

Systems unit. *Personal computer hardware* that holds the *CPU*, the *disk drives* and the hard disk.

Terminal. A *hardware* device that receives or sends *data* to a computer.

Transistor. A device that switches electricity on or off.

User interface. The *hardware* and *software* systems which allow a user to communicate with their computer.

Virtual reality. Computer technology that creates the illusion of a 3-D world, which users can feel they are part of.

Virus. A *program* which is written deliberately to damage or destroy *data*. Viruses can pass from one computer to another via *networks* or *disks*.

Wide area network (WAN). A *network* of computers spread over a large geographical area.

Write to. The process of storing *data* on a storage device, such as a *floppy disk*.

Index

A

address, 8, 44
address bus, 5
Altair, 6
analytical engine, 38
anti-glare screen, 40
anti-virus software, 32
Apple, 7
applications software, 10, 12-
    13, 21, 44
arithmetic unit, 3, 44
assembler program, 35, 44
automated teller machines, 27

B

Babbage, Charles, 38, 39
backing up, 41, 44
banks, 27
bar codes, 23
battleships, computer, 5
binary code, 4, 16, 35, 38, 44
binary digits, 4
bits, 4, 8, 44
bloodstream, 22
books, 25
"booting up" process, 8, 10,
    11
brain (human), 3, 14, 22, 37
bugs, 34, 44
buses, 5, 44
bytes, 4, 5, 8, 44

C

calculating machines, 38, 39
capacity, 9
cartoons, 28
Cascade virus, 33
cash dispensing machines, 27
CAT scanners, 22
cathode ray monitor, 16, 17
cathode ray tube (CRT), 16, 44
CD drive, 28, 42
CD-ROM, 28, 29, 42
Central Processing Unit (CPU),
    3, 5, 8, 9, 11, 14, 15, 16,
    19, 20, 23, 28, 44
    CPU chip, 4
charge-coupled devices
    (CCDs), 15
chess, 36, 37

chips, 4, 5, 44
    as firmware, 11
    development of, 6, 39
color monitors, 16, 17, 42
compact discs (CD), 28-29,
    42, 44
compiler program, 35, 44
computer-aided design (CAD),
    24
computer error, 3
computer operators, 20
computer programmer, 21, 38
control bus, 5
control unit, 3, 44
cursor, 14, 44

D

daisy wheel printer, 18
data, 3, 10, 15, 18, 24, 27,
    28, 44
    and binary digits, 4
    and crime, 32
    and databases, 12
    and disks, 9, 28
    and memory, 8
data bus, 5
data compression, 29, 44
data gloves, 30
data processing (DP), 20
database, 7, 12, 13, 23, 44
database administrators, 20
daughterboards, 5
decimal numbers, 38, 44
desktop publishing (DTP), 25
digital, 44
directories, 11, 41
disassembler program, 35, 44
discs,
    compact, 28-29, 42, 44
    optical, 28-29, 45
disks,
    floppy, 9, 10, 12, 32, 41,
    42, 44
    hard, 9, 10, 11, 12, 32,
    41, 42, 44
    magnetic, 9, 28
disk drives, 9, 44
    care of, 41
    floppy, 6, 41, 42
    hard, 6, 9

disk hub, 9
dot matrix printer, 18
drugs, 22

E

earphones (virtual reality), 30
Eckert, Presper, 39
electronic (definition), 44
electronic circuits, 4, 11, 39
electronic keyboard, 5
electronic mail (e-mail), 26,
    27, 42, 44
electronic pulses, (see pulses)
electrons, 16
encryption, 44
ENIAC, 39
EPCOT Center, 15
erasable optical discs, 28
espionage, 33

F

feature analysis, 15
field (in a database), 12
file, 11, 13, 44
file server, 26
film, 16, 25
firing chambers, 18
firmware, 11
flat screen monitors, 17
flight simulator, 30
floppy disk, 9, 10, 12, 32, 41,
    44
floppy disk drive, 6, 41
fonts, 25
forecasting, 13
format, 44
fractals, 24
function keys, 14, 44
fusing unit, 19

G

gigabytes, 9, 44
graphics, 3, 7, 16, 18, 24, 25,
    29, 30, 42, 44
GUI, 44
Gulf War, 33

H

hackers, 32, 33, 44
hard copy, 16, 18, 44
hard disk, 9, 10, 11, 12, 32, 41, 42, 44
hard disk drive, 6, 9
hardware, 3, 10, 20, 44
  buying hardware, 42
  care of, 41
  input hardware, 14-15
  output hardware, 16-19
headsets (virtual reality), 30, 31
health, 40
high-level languages, 35, 44

I

IBM, 7
icon, 44
information section, 20
information technology, 45
inkjet printer, 18
input, 3, 4, 14, 45
input hardware, 5, 14-15
instruction manuals, 12, 41
integrated circuits, 45
integrated software, 13, 43
interface, 45
Internet, 27, 29, 42
interpreter program, 35, 45
iron oxide, 9
ISDN, 45

K

keyboard, 6, 7, 10, 11, 14, 20, 40, 42
keyboard operators, 20
kilobytes, 45

L

lands, 28
languages, computer, 35
laser beam, 19, 23, 28
laser printer, 19, 45
librarians, 20
light emitting diodes (LEDs), 14
light pen, 45
liquid crystal display (LCD), 17
local area networks (LANs), 26, 45
logic gates, 4, 45
Lovelace, Ada, 38

low-level languages, 35, 45

M

machine code, 45
Macintosh, 7
magazines, 25
magnetic disks, 9, 28
magnetic tape, 9
mainframes, 6, 20-21, 23, 33, 45
maintenance engineers, 20
Maltese Amoeba virus, 32
matrix matching, 15
Mauchly, John, 39
medicine, 22, 31
megabytes, 9, 45
memory, 3, 5, 15, 19, 45
  cells, 8
  and character recognition, 15
  chips, 4, 5
  RAM, 8, 9, 11, 35, 45
  ROM, 8, 10, 11, 45
menu, 14
Michelangelo virus, 32
Microsoft Windows, 10
milking system, robotic, 22
minicomputer, 45
MIPS, 45
missiles, 23
modem, 27, 42, 45
monitors, 3, 6, 7, 40, 45
  care of, 41
  cathode ray, 16
  flat screen, 17
  LCD, 17
  monochrome, 17
monsters, 21
Morse Code, 4
motherboard, 5, 6, 45
mouse, 6, 7, 11, 14, 29, 40, 45
multimedia presentations, 29, 42
music, 17, 28

N

networks, computer, 26-27, 45
  and crime, 32, 33
newspapers, 25
notepads, 7, 45
notebook computers, 7, 45

O

on-line, 27
operating system, 10, 11
operations section, 20
optical character readers (OCRs), 15
optical disc, 28, 45
oscillator, 17
output, 3, 16, 19, 45
output hardware, 5, 16-19

P

painting software, 24
PDAs, 7, 45
passwords, 21
peripheral, 45
personal computers, 6-7, 11, 13, 15, 21, 23, 26, 28, 45
  and your health, 40
  buying a PC, 42-43
  history of, 6
pirating, 32
pits, 28
pixel, 16, 45
portable computers, 7, 17
posture, 40
pressure pads (virtual reality), 30
print spooler, 19
printed circuit boards (PCBs), 4, 45
printer, 10, 16, 18-19, 20, 42
  daisy wheel, 18
  dot matrix, 18
  ink jet, 18
  laser, 19
printer driver, 19
processing unit, 3
programming section, 21
programs, 3, 6, 8, 10, 11, 12, 24, 34, 35, 45
  and crime, 32
pulses, 4, 9, 27, 28, 38
punched cards, 38

R

Random-Access Memory (RAM), 8, 9, 11, 35, 45
read from, 45
reading text, 15
Read-Only Memory (ROM), 8, 10, 11, 45
read-only optical disc, 28

read/write heads, 9
record (in a database), 13
repetitive strain syndrome
    (RSS), 40
resolution, 45
robots, 5, 22, 31, 36

S

satellites, 23, 26, 27, 31
saving, 45
scanners, 15, 45
    bar code, 23
screen, 10, 14, 15, 16, 20
screen saver, 41
shadow mask, 16
Shanks, William, 39
silicon, 45
silicon chips, (see chips)
soft copy, 16
software, 3, 10, 17, 21, 22, 27,
    41, 45
    applications software, 12-13
    buying software, 41, 42-43
    operating system, 10-11

painting software, 24
sound, 29
sound card, 42
sound software, 17
sound synthesizer, 17
speakers, 42
speech synthesis, 17
spellcheck, 11
spreadsheet, 7, 13, 45
supercomputers, 21
support services, 43
swapping, 11
systems analysis section, 20
systems analysts, 21
systems unit, 6, 45

T

telephone lines, 26, 27, 33
telephone numbers, 23
terminals, computer, 20, 23,
    26, 27, 45
touchscreens, 15
transistors, 39, 45
typesetting, 25

U

utilities, 11

V

valves, 39
video, 29, 31
virtual reality, 30-31, 45
viruses, computer, 32, 45

W

washing machine, 5
wide area networks (WANs),
    27, 45
WIMPS, 45
word processing, 7, 12, 13, 43
write-once, read-many optical
    disc (WORM), 28
write-protect tab, 9
write to, 45

X Z

X-rays, 22
Zuse, Konrad, 38

Acknowledgements

The publishers are grateful to the following organizations
for permission to reproduce their material:
Front cover: central computer - Western Systems Ltd;
(clockwise from top right) Sharp Electronics (UK) Ltd; Alfred Pasieka/Science Photo Library;
Usborne Publishing Ltd; Autodesk Ltd; Usborne Publishing Ltd; Rainbow Technologies Ltd; Thomas
Porett/Science Photo Library; Sharp Electronics (UK) Ltd
p4. Ferranti Electronics/A. Sternberg/Science Photo Library
p7. Sharp Electronics (UK) Ltd
p17. Sharp Electronics (UK) Ltd
p22. (Artist's reference for robotic milking system) Silsoe Research Institute
p23. ©Crown copyright 1994/MOD. Reproduced with the permission of the Controller of HMSO.
p24. (CAD plane) Autodesk Ltd. (Fractal) Alfred Pasieka/Science Photo Library
(Face) Thomas Porett/Science Photo Library

First published in 1994 and revised in 1997 by Usborne Publishing Ltd, Usborne House,
83-85 Saffron Hill, London, EC1N 8RT, England.